I Had A Really Great Title, But Now I Can't Remember It

(Poems for the Older Generation)

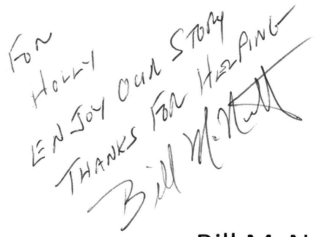

For Holly
Enjoy our story
Thanks for helping
Bill McNulty

Bill McNulty

Table of Contents

Introduction

People within my "older" generation are living longer, and while hopefully all of us find worthy activities to fill our days, we are not without our issues. There are health concerns for many of us, and times we complain or listen to our friends complain. Memory problems can strike in a variety of ways and illnesses.

Of course, everyone handles aging in his or her own way. Some have admirably determined to keep living as they always did. Many show their age, while others age far more gracefully. Some have family that surrounds them, and others age all alone. Loved ones, family, friends and neighbors disappear from our lives and we don't always handle it well.

I'm sharing many poems in this this book that try to have a little fun with issues of aging (the same could be said for the title). Please know I would never intend to offend anyone—laughter, as they say, is the best medicine! But mostly, I hope these poems challenge all of us to get more out of life.

I'm also including some notes on resources, to help better meet the challenges of aging. These notes are only an introduction and I urge you to investigate the options online to get full and current details.

For a variety of reasons, I often think of my parents and in-laws. There was much that I learned from all four of them. As the years pass, I find myself, and my wife, Susan, quoting our parents. Now we give them credit for some of the life-lessons that we learned. For that reason, you will see pages in here dedicated to them.

This collection was penned with the hope of entertaining you and at the same time, raising some funds for Alzheimer's research. Alzheimer's is a terrible disease that affects everyone connected to it.

I have one more request: That older relative or friend that you were going to visit and just have not found the time? Make the time. Make a date and go visit for an hour.

When I started this book, I wanted to include the perspective of someone who deals with the reality of Alzheimer's on a daily basis. I reached out to my niece, Carrie, and asked her for thoughts on this dreaded disease. Her response in this message illustrates the concerns, struggles and fears:

You very kindly and thoughtfully reached out to me a few months ago and asked me if I'd like to contribute anything about my experience with my mom.

I am typically very responsible about deadlines and commitments, so I've been struggling with why I've taken so long to respond. I have shared bits and pieces via social media about Dementia and Alzheimer's, so why is it a challenge to share more?

I've come to multiple reasons/excuses...

This is a family disease, and we've always been fairly private about our daily struggles with my mom. It's a disease where the family and loved one (mom) are often isolated and feel alone. Many family members and friends are uncomfortable inquiring how we are doing. I know now it's because most just don't know what to say. I've come to accept this as time has gone on, and my frustration has turned to understanding. We as a family feel uncomfortable at times, so why should we want others to feel that way?

I've learned a great deal on this journey. First of all, it is the longest and saddest goodbye. Most gather their information about this terrible disease through what they've seen in films. Let me just say, to meet one person with Alzheimer's is to meet one person with Alzheimer's. There are some universal truths, but every individual's experience is unique to them. The path on a yearly, monthly, weekly, daily spiral down is excruciating.

I've learned when you become the parent to your parent, the transition can be difficult. Once you realize what your new role is, you do the best you can to always keep their best interests at heart. Give them a quality of life, maintain their dignity. You do your best to not negate or deny their reality.

As an actress and an acting teacher, I teach (and was taught) to always stay in the moment. You tell the story as authentically as you can, always going moment to moment. You never want to get ahead or fall behind your audience. I've put this into practice when I'm with my mom. I am patient, gentle, and completely focused on her needs. I need to repeat things over and over and over again. I try to stay in her world of needs. It is not her fault that she forgot what I just said. We may go over the same thing multiple times over the course of 5 minutes. 2 minutes later, the same thing again. Breathe. Repeat. Go moment to moment.

I've been asked many times if my mom still knows who we are. I've gotten better about not getting annoyed about that. People who are fortunate enough to not have someone they love go through this heart wrenching disease simply do not know. The disease is much more complicated than that. I also wish we could remove the shame and fear associated with this disease. We must spread awareness, but understandably we are afraid.

I can say I've lost many a night's sleep worrying about my mom. Selfishly, I've lived with a great deal of fear that I'll end up just like her.

I love my mom. I miss my mom. Even though she's still on this earth, I miss her. When I visit with her, or take her out to eat, or to a movie. I miss her. We hug, and I tell her I love her so much. When I look into her eyes, I miss her.

I'm deeply sorry it took me so long to unlock a part of me and share more with you.

Much love, Carrie

Chapter One: Aging

The challenges of aging surround us. Those that have attained that golden age, regardless of the number of years, have different approaches to the life they lead.

That group approaching old age has questions and concerns: Do I retire or continue to work? Where will I live? What changes will I have to make regarding health, or finances?

Somewhere in the aging process, we go from no aches and pains that bother us to every creaky knee or minor infection giving us grief. Aging is not always graceful.

The poems in this chapter portray a variety of themes. I hope they will make you think. Perhaps they will make you question where you are in life. I certainly hope you find a line that will make you laugh. And if not a laugh, may there be a slight chuckle, or a smile on your face.

When Tomorrow Is Gone

When did tomorrow become yesterday?
Did all those todays get in the way?
Plans we make just go astray,
Clear dreams become very gray.
Projects not done that are within our reach,
Become a lesson that is so easy to teach.
Before you know it, ten years just vanish,
And what can you say you did accomplish?
No time to wonder what I will have missed,
If I don't start on today's "to do" list.

So When Are We Old?

Not as long as there are new adventures to seek.
Not as long as we enjoy each day of every week.
Not as long as we can still welcome family and friends.
Not as long as we keep reading to see how the story ends.
Not as long as there are new poems and lyrics to create.
Not as long as there is still love to share with your mate.
Not as long as there are children and grandchildren to hug.
Not as long as there are ways they give your heart a tug.
Not as long as there are still emotions that let you shed a tear.
Not as long as with your annual exam, doctor says see you next year.

A Walk Through Life

From the tentative first steps of a baby,
To the faltering steps of an old man trying to still be.
We walk through life in so many ways,
Never knowing what events may limit our days.
You watch the running of a young boy's mad dash.
Soon it becomes the swagger of a young man so brash.
You see a young girl's first steps in high heels trying to balance.
Now, she's a young woman with a model's walkway prance.
Years later, the steps are slower and not as sure.
Any pain-free morning with no Advil is now a treasure.

The Joys of Aging

So here I am not feeling well today.
How I am doing, is not for me to say.
Sorry, I have to go to the bathroom without delay.
I'm back, pardon me if my old mind does stray.
And which med am I to take when I wake?
Speak UP, I can't hear you, for heaven's sake!
Stop at Walgreen's to pick up another med.
I think I take that one before I go to bed.
My knees ache, so maybe some ice and Ben Gay.
It's not so easy, getting older and really gray.
Did I tell you about my lower back strain?
But who am I to sit here and really complain?

Creaky Knees

These old knees really do creak.
It seems to hurt more each week.
Turn the wrong way, it gives me grief.
Advil, ice pack, please give me relief.
What new ointment should we try today?
Any new damage showing on the x-ray?
Now an injection with some new gel.
Walk too much and either knee may swell.
My legs don't always properly engage.
As I have reached this point, called old age.

These Aging Eyes

Older eyes and the print is tougher to read.
The perils of getting old, I must concede.
Now those books with the larger print,
To you, are now worth a tidy mint.
A longer arm helps you see it all.
When you can't read it, just stall.
There are no decent replies,
So you just close your eyes.
Suddenly all is all right because...
A curvy beauty just brings all into focus.

What Memories?

At what age do stairs get higher and aisles longer?
I certainly remember being a lot stronger.
Remember how quickly you used to get down stairs?
Now you look at the steps and say, who cares.
Can you remember when your eyes covered quite a distance?
And now your poor eyes give you total resistance.
Do you remember how easy it was to ties your shoes?
Now whenever you can, it's slip-ons and loafers you choose.
Of course, most of what I remember is questionable.
But then most of what I can still do is laughable.

The Autumn of Our Life

As you age, so often, your memory begins to fade,
You struggle to remember all the plans that you made.
Now there are days you feel like an empty shell,
Because you can't recall faces you know so well.
Question it, when is there the memory card to play?
When thoughts disappear and you don't know what to say.
Movie titles that helped you win many a game,
Now you can't remember a movie star's name.
You look to your spouse for a possible clue,
Perhaps, she will know just what to do.
At times, we all wonder just how will we handle old age,
Work at making it not the last chapter, just another page.

A Senior View

You know that your steps have slowed down.
It's tougher and tougher to get around town.
Believe it when I say that I have found,
I have gained more than an extra pound.
So it should be no surprise,
That I am now a larger size.
And when I get up, my back does ache.
No doubt, there is more Advil to take.
Shoulders are now stooped and bent.
My energy is quickly drained and spent.
Hearing and eyesight is questionable.
So far, my mind is still able.
As long as my mind and body last,
I will make every year a total blast.

Those Without Names

You see a face, but there is no name.
Try as you may, there is no connection to claim.
Some names seem so easy to place.
Some names, so easy, with a given face.
Others, no matter how you try, are a total blank.
For whatever reason, in your mind, they don't rank.
You repeat names when you meet someone.
Look for a connection when the meeting is done.
And what is the next move when a name is not in sight?
Until you remember, you will not sleep tonight.

Early Bird Specials

You will never have to ask me twice,
When the dinner menu says half-price.
The early bird specials are on the board,
All of them priced so you can easily afford.
Early bird specials say where you will have dinner.
Eat out every night, and you'll never get thinner.
Do you look for those early bird specials to dine out?
Those that do, certainly know what deals are about.
At any time, at any age, and in every single state,
Specials abound, assuming you don't arrive late.

Worth the Wait

Another forehead wrinkle found today.
That thinning hairline is still turning gray.
Those reflexes are slower than they used to be.
I squint and blink to clear my eyes to see.
More than ever there's an extra washroom trip,
Where you stand and wait for another drip, drip, drip.
Every year, there are more meds to take.
Those extra naps are helping me stay awake.
To heighten your senses and justify your worst fears,
My driver's license was renewed for another four years.

Doctor Visit

Back to the doctor, and the nurse is there to meet and greet,
As she sweetly hands you more forms to complete.
You sit and wait for your appointment time,
Working on another line of poetry to rhyme.
Others sit and read a magazine from last year.
Some talk about the appointment and what they fear.
Will the doctor be on time or running late?
Check your watch; how long can you wait?
As your notebook rests on your lap,
I just close my eyes and take a nap.

Slowing Down

You know that you are slower than you used to be.
Maybe it's time to rest under that old shade tree.
More time is needed to do the simple and routine.
Your potbelly is more than should ever be seen.
Those old bones really do ache and creak.
When did I get old and suddenly so weak?
In the past year, it's so easy to get sick.
At this age, you don't recover so quick.
Trying to remember when I was in good shape.
Maybe that was when we played that 8-track tape.
The days are long gone when I used to run.
I still exercise, but am so happy when I'm done.

Chapter Two: Memories

There are some memories that fade away and others stay so vivid in our mind. Are some more special than others?

I know that some of us would like a "do over" on events in our lives. Of course, we are looking for a different outcome. There will always be an occurrence that we would like to forget. Many of us, gathered for the same event, remember it very differently. Time and perception make interesting discussions in later years.

There is something special about how we remember the growing-up days of our youth. We don't always remember it the same way as our siblings or friends.

Hopefully, this group of poems will touch your thoughts, feelings and memories.

Hold On

We hold on to sweet memories of long ago.
Hoping that whatever we don't know won't show.
We hold on to words that our Mother would say.
But so many memories are gone from yesterday.
Pictures in our mind are not always easy to find.
For some, the passing years are not very kind.
We hold on to those lessons learned in first grade.
And all those friendships that we would never trade.
And to Good Health, we hold on tight.
As age reduces our hearing and eyesight.
Hold on to all those pictures and stories,
That helped create all those memories.

When I Was Younger

I remember the old days.
In B Ball, I made all the plays.
In those days, the movies were 25 cents.
People still seemed to have common sense.
When I was younger, it all seemed so easy.
Working and planning on who I wanted to be.
When I could still bend and touch my toes.
When there was no E. D. on TV shows.
When I didn't worry about what I ate.
When it was no problem staying up late.
I remember all the streets in the old neighborhood.
Where everyone behaved as they knew they should.
Those days with better eyesight and a steady hand.
Those days with music with a singer and a big band.
And from your younger days what do you recall?
Those days when we were young and knew it all.

Looking Back

As you look back at life, what would you like to do again?
What did you accomplish that rates a perfect ten?
Was it really easier in the old days?
What do we recall from all those yesterdays?
I can see the park in the old neighborhood.
To go back and play ball again, if only I could.
Choices that we made so many years ago,
Looking back, I wonder what I really did know.
I wonder if a different school choice was made,
Could I really have attained a better grade?
Work decisions, so easy to second guess.
I've done it many times, I must confess.
Often, we all look back,
To see if our life is still on track.

Mama's Rules

Mama's rules from long ago always stay with us.
You better obey or Mama could really make a fuss.
There were rules on how and where to shop.
And rules on when to eat and when to stop.
If homework was done early, you got to play a game.
Clothes? Turned inside out, washed and returned the same.
Dishwasher rules: knife point-down or you got stuck.
Watch your words at dinner or it would cost you a buck.
And all the stories that you will NEVER tell your kid,
About the crazy rules that your mother had and did.

Baseball from the Old Days

America's pastime, they used to say.
Players showed up to play every day.
Back then, baseball was a different game.
Those fans knew every player's name.
In the bleachers, where we all loved to sit,
We would cheer our favorites coming up to hit.
Ballpark hot dogs and snacks, we ate to excess.
Every manager and ump was ours to second-guess.
No TV replays to tell you safe or out.
The ump's call was it, done right, never a doubt.
The basics of pitch, hit, catch and throw are still the same.
But in my younger days, it sure seemed like a different game.

Memories of Our Parents

Certain things about our parents, we can never forget.
There were expectations that should be met.
Always there for every ball game.
There to cheer and shout your name.
And when you were small and in their care.
There were always family stories to share.
There was always a present on your birthday.
Always be respectful in everything you say.
So many family memories that are oh, so sweet.
So many phrases they used, we often repeat.
The years have gone by much too fast.
Parents to children, memories that will last.

I would wager most of us remember the first car that we learned how to drive. Was it stick shift? Can you remember the color? No doubt there are some memories that we cannot describe in this book. There are even some who can still recall the details of the automobiles of decades ago.

Cars from Our Younger Days

Remember all those cars of our younger days?
Autos we still talk about with great praise.
All those young ladies with lessons to teach,
Park and watch sub races at Montrose beach.
Remember your dream car that you loved to drive,
You drive and accelerate and you really felt alive.
For date night, there was dad's Coupe DeVille.
Maybe it was the Camero that gave you a thrill.
For friends, you had to talk to and explain,
Why you loved that old Ford Fairlane.
You tuned up the engine and it really sang,
When you revved the engine on your Ford Mustang.
And there was the Olds sedan with the big back seat,
With the sexy blond who could really turn up the heat.
Wasn't there a muscle car model called Spitfire,
With every possible feature that you could desire?
Who could forget the old red Corvette?
Hit the gas and collect on any dollar bet.
Do you remember your first ticket or accident?
And how did your parents react to the incident?
Oh yes, we remember the VW bug and muscle cars,
And cruising in the convertible under the stars.
All the latest model cars may have more wonderful toys,
But nothing replaces the memories of cars when we were boys.

Music of Our Younger Days

When did Big Band music go Rock N Roll?
Remember the dance floor doing the stroll?
Up the tempo and pick up the beat.
On the edge of your seat, tapping your feet.
The horn section with all the energy they could bring,
Helped define the music of the times they called swing.
Thinking of the music and stars of long ago.
The music on the radio became a TV variety show.
The records of songs that we loved to play.
Gone, but not forgotten music of yesterday.

Hot Dog Memories

From the push cart on old Maxwell Street.
To any hot dog place where you love to eat.
To hit all those taste buds you can bring,
Step up to the counter and order yours with everything.
Who could know there are so many blogs?
Detailing all those ways to eat your hot dogs.
Your Red Hot can be charred or steamed.
With all the toppings that you have dreamed.
Just so you don't forget and mess up,
It's Chicago, so don't even think about ketchup.

The Memories That Stay with Us

Sometimes we think about our days as a young boy.
Often those memories are something special to still enjoy.
Time passes, some memories fade, some memories stay.
There are some images so special that you must hit replay.
Some memories are there to give you a big grin.
As you remember your team, with a big upset win.
Sunsets over water always seem brand new.
Rainbows filling our sky are always a special view.
Words that touch me and I hope touch you, too.
Our grandchild's goodbye, bye Grandpa, I love you.

A Poem for Dad

You look at the chair where he used to sit.
I liked to visit when time would permit.
Guitar strumming, he loved to play.
I remember it like it was yesterday.
Playing sports or trumping your ace,
If he won, you heard it every place.
At times, thinking about him, I get the blues.
Still today, I want to call him and share good news.
When needed, he gave you everything he had.
At this hour, in this season, I really miss my dad.

Reunion Tribute

Decades ago, you left high school behind.
Soon a reunion, with old classmates to find.
Some no longer with us, who will you miss?
How about that girl, who shared your first kiss.
What friends were in the morning study hall?
Who was on the team when you played ball?
Freshman to senior, the years went by so fast.
Many of those friendships were made to last.
Can you remember the old school song?
If I start the chorus, can you sing along?
All those memories from so long ago.
I'm going to see who I still know.

Title, Unknown

I remember lines from a song long ago.
Who sang the song, I should know.
Was it a Broadway melody or country tune?
Give me a few minutes—I'll remember it soon.
The music stays in my head, the title does not.
I can hum the tune, but the title I forgot.
Some catchy tunes just stay in my mind.
It's the old song title I cannot find.
Those same lyrics keep going through my head,
I should Google that title before I go to bed.

The Old Neighborhood

Sometimes it's fun to tour the old neighborhood,
Remembering who lived on which block, when I could.
The bistro that we enjoyed on the square,
The grocery store that is no longer there.
Twenty years since we lived on that avenue,
No neighbors are there that we once knew.
The trees changing color every fall.
The park where the kids played ball.
The friends that we met down the street.
The ice cream parlor that we went for a treat.
Now, we all may be getting older, wrinkled and a little gray,
Thinking about the old house, makes it seem like yesterday.

Chapter Three: Next Chapter

As you age, you move on to the next chapter in life. You become an in-law, with a new daughter or son to add to your family. Before you know it, you are a grandparent. Grandchildren are born and there is that instant love that needs no explanation.

With more time, you volunteer. Those volunteers are always needed and new connections are made with others who also volunteer. There will always be something rewarding about making a difference in the world we live in.

Communication today brings new challenges, especially when it comes to technology. Most frustrating is when you master the program you are using, and they update or change it so you have to learn to master it again.

Grandma's Brag Book

There's something about Grandma's Brag Book,
That always makes you want to take another look.
A granddaughter's story that she often repeats.
Grandma seems to tell the story to all she meets.
And if that young student gets a perfect score,
Grandma tells it like it's never been done before.
If there's a headline that your grandchild can bag,
You know the grandparent will post a Facebook Brag.
And if your grandchild becomes a doctor, by chance.
It's a story Grandma will tell and greatly enhance.
Be prepared when all her pictures come out,
For Grandma will lovingly share, without a doubt.

The Role of Grandpa

The role of Grandfather is easy to play:
Figure out what is needed on any given day.
When they are young, there's bedtime stories to share,
There's always a princess to rescue from the dragon's lair.
So many games to play but what will the kids choose?
Your whole role is to smile, play and gracefully lose.
You must always attend your grandchild's concert.
To celebrate, you take her out to share your favorite dessert.
As they grow, you are no longer needed to babysit.
To play ball, you help him break in his new baseball mitt.
You know—we all know—your best role, as all can see:
Make sure that Grandma is always content and happy.

Those Older Volunteers

Often you can watch older volunteers giving back.
In some ways, keeping the next generation on track.
Always there to share what they know.
Doing their best, to never let spirits get low.
One morning a week, teaching children to read.
Coaching them how and when to take the lead.
At any hospital, older volunteers helping out.
They assist patients of any age to get about.
Helping to make sure no one's cupboard is bare.
Their love of hobbies and talents to always share.
Given the chance, they will help you always explore,
Paths to make the community better than it was before.

Still the Wish to Play

YES, we old guys can still hit the ball.
But these old legs don't let us run at all.
And first base seems so far away.
I'd need Advil to help me play today.
Age 65, to sign up and play,
Brings me back to the fields of yesterday.
Can hit, can throw and catch, just can't run.
Still, trying to compete will always be fun.
No skill, but the game has always appealed.
Whatever you do, don't play me in the outfield.
Out of shape and some would say fat.
But I still want one last time at bat.

With Dignity and Respect

So how will the older generation be treated?
Walking in the door, how will they be greeted?
The grandmother that you love and adore,
Be there when she needs you to open a door.
Be there when she needs you to go to the store.
When a kind word is needed, give that and more.
The older person that you meet on the street,
Courtesy and a polite nod for all that you meet.
And when you reach that age, what would you expect?
Your role today: treat them with dignity and respect.

Old Friends

Sometimes it's fun to gather with the old crew.
How is everyone doing and what's new?
How are the kids and where are you off to next year?
What about the old guy, what gossip do you hear?
Any stories to share that won't embarrass you too much?
Did I tell you what I heard when I met friends for lunch?
Keeping up with old friends, through good times and bad,
Always there for comfort when I am smiling or just sad.
Pictures to post and a vacation post card to send,
With a greeting that always starts, "Dear Friend".
For next year we say, travel safe, good health and be well.
May there be meals to share and more stories to tell.

The Computer Age

What used to go on paper now goes on your laptop.
When you need something, it's the Internet to shop.
Passwords to remember, better write them down.
Check Google, so you know where to go in town.
To stay current, you must learn how to update.
Need the latest version to remain first rate.
You learn what's on the Internet isn't always true.
You master Facebook to keep up with your crew.
Today, you smile and you are so proud,
You now store your pictures in a cloud.
When you are trying to figure what comes next,
Learn how to send your grandchild another text.

Senior Upgrade

Another email message saying it's time to upgrade.
As an elder, this note always makes me afraid.
This upgrade offers your system more speed.
A security warning that you really must heed.
Learn about hackers that have a certain greed.
So much technical verbiage that you never can read.
Upgrade, and the options that I use have been moved.
All those changes, I would never have approved.
New options and features that seem so strange,
Would not be a problem if I didn't make a change.

Chapter Four: Reflections

Sometimes a reflection. Sometimes a wish. Sometimes a prayer.

I look back at events in my life and wonder, what did I learn? I can look back and wish that I made a better effort at a given task. Often I pray for future generations in wishing them the ability to solve the issues we passed on to them. There is much we all take for granted. How often do you hear or say, "I should have…"

Moving On

When shadows fall and clouds darken your day,
When new problems challenge your way,
Living your daily life can always be a test.
Places to be when you are not at your best.
You learn new ways to manage and cope,
Even when you accept there is no hope.
A time to remember and a time to forget,
A time to move forward with no regret.
Sometimes we are at a loss,
For why we feel and act so cross.
Life moves on and so should we.
Never perfect, I'm sure we agree.

Turning Point

Can you identify a turning point in your life?
Was it a celebration or time of great strife?
Was there a loss that still resides in your heart?
Was there a birth that puts joy in the same heart?
Were there words from years past,
With Solomon advice that will always last?
Were there life decisions that we, or others, made,
That paint pictures in your mind that will never fade?
Perhaps it was a special life discovery that you didn't expect.
It will create building blocks for a life to lead with great respect.
Are we ever aware of where that turning point may be?
That shapes our lives and determines our destiny.

An Old Man's Prayer

During our life, we pray for many things,
With all the success or failure that it brings.
That everything is done on my "to do" list.
That when I am gone, I will be missed.
That once in a while, my children heed my advice.
That all the nations in turmoil learn to play nice.
That every day I will remember to take my meds.
That my words are worthy enough to stay in reader's heads.
That the plane I'm on will safely touch down.
That all is well with loved ones in our home town.
That medical research offers cures for what our kids will face.
That hatred and bigotry will disappear from earth without a trace.
That when we reach the next world, whenever it may be.
There will be lasting peace on which we all can agree.
There is always spirted teamwork that will prevail,
On every ship of hopeful dreams that set sail.
May there always be innovations and benefits to share and sell.
For me, may there always be another chapter of life to tell.

Is Life a Test?

Isn't all of life a serious test,
Deciding which choice will work best?
Driver's license, school exam, who to wed?
Choose this player, NO, take me instead!
Fantasy Football Pool, what odds are set?
Now will all your expectations be met?
What foods to eat when there are pounds to lose?
A little less means lost pounds or really good news.
Are there times when decisions are not your choice?
It's time to step up, step in, and raise your voice.
Yes, living life will always be the ultimate test.
Just do it right and you will never be stressed.

Time to Reflect

Some call it Zen Time, or time for me.
Time to think about all you are expected to be.
Decisions you have made you want to correct.
Different life choices that may not intersect.
Does your worship offer you a silent prayer,
Where you look for guidance for those in your care?
Or sitting in your backyard, listening to nature's call,
Wondering if you really have any answers at all.
Should you start a project or let it go?
Is it the right call, only you will know.
Maybe if I take a walk, my problems will disappear.
Sometimes our mind has to shift into a slower gear.
There will always be new adventures to find.
So always have time and space to clear your mind.

DNA Report

What's so special about your DNA?
Can you tell us what it has to say?
Time after time, there's a story to tell.
All because of one genetic cell.
We all long to have that creativity gene.
As we all want to be the best talent ever seen.
My daddy's baby blues could be the color of my eyes.
Who knows the number of years the longevity gene buys?
There just may be a genetic trait,
That seals your lifeline fate.

Staying Calm

So how much stress is there in your life?
How do you plan to handle all this strife?
Sometimes you just have to sit and watch the sunset.
Make time for you to recharge, which you won't regret.
Problems that you have won't magically disappear.
But it can always help to share with a friendly ear.
You can read or write or share a glass of wine.
Find a place that's yours with no need to define.
There will always be issues for you to address.
But we all need that time to rest with no stress.

As so many of the older generation served, I wanted to include words I wrote for Memorial Day in 2014. We honor and respect all those who serve and protect, in any generation.

Memorial Day

Memorial Day, are there lost friends to fondly remember?
Someone special who was an Armed Forces member?
We honor our lost soldiers with parades and songs,
They journeyed the world to battle evil and wrongs.
Do we value the freedom we have because of those that serve?
They faced foreign elements with courage and nerve.
Sometimes we wonder what history will say,
About the wars and conflicts we fought today.
We cover many a coffin with red, white and blue,
Trying to honor fallen heroes with their due.
Never take for granted the rights and freedoms we enjoy,
Those freedoms are ours, because of many a soldier girl or boy.

Chapter Five: A Personal Perspective

Here we offer the words of someone with an intimate connection to dementia and Alzheimer's disease. Hopefully, there is a verse or two that offer understanding of the daily struggle that family and caretakers must face. If you smile, cry or say, "I can relate to that", then these words have done their job.

*All the poems in this section are from **Melissa Conner**, who writes from personal experience as a daughter witnessing her mother progressing with dementia. In her verses, Melissa captures the perspectives of both mother and daughter.*

A Story Told Again and Again...

A story told again and again,
Who knows where, who knows when.
A misplaced item – a key, a phone
A smack to the forehead, a grunt, a moan.
Misplaced glasses in a bed of hair
"I knew I had them – they were just right there!"
A story told again and again,
Who knows where, who knows when.
Orange juice in the bowl, milk in the glass,
A story told...just let it pass.
Body and mind – finding Zen.
Who knows where, who knows when.
"Did I ever tell you..."? YES YOU DID.
Inner voice: "Be patient, kid."
A story told again and again,
Who knows where, who knows when.
A story told again and again,
Who knows where, who knows when.
Dodging the inevitable juggernaut,
A laugh because that's all we've got.

Sulfur

I see the flicker,
It shines behind her eyes when she sees something she should know
A face...
A place...
A name...
The match strikes,
Then fizzles.
Sulfur.

A Daughter's Sonnet

Back in the day we would talk for hours
A pot of coffee brewing on the stove.
Talking about life among the flowers
Listening to birds from the nearby grove.
Now it's a struggle to just sit and talk,
Watching the wheels of her brain slowly turn.
Sometimes her sentences are poppycock
It's like a whole different language to learn.
My mom's a child I'll never outgrow
Conversations are like a pantomime.
Thoughts blowing around like a tornado
Watching her brain slowly move back in time.
She's just too young to be in this mindset
But perhaps, more so, too young to forget.

I'm Still Here

I can't remember the date or time
I can't remember the reason or rhyme
I may not be able to recite Shakespeare
But I'm still here.
I may not be able to cook or clean
I may come across as hostile or mean
But please be patient and lend me an ear
Because I'm still here.
Sometimes I can't tell my left from my right
Or be able to tell if my shirt is too tight
Sometimes I may not remember my peers
But I'm still here.
The memories fly like a fast-moving plane
Jetting through the puffy clouds in my brain
Here and gone, quick as a deer
But I'm still here.
The days turn to weeks inside my head
"What was it that you just said?"
For whatever reason the names don't adhere
But I'm still here.
I feel myself forgetting names
Simple descriptions fall out of frame
Sometimes I'm scared that I'll disappear
But, for now, I'm here.

Hide and Seek

Some people think my brain is blank
Air blowing around in a vast, empty tank
But the facts and the figures play hide-and-seek in my head
Looming behind dark corners instead.
Who knows what I'm bound to find
When I'm searching in the deep corners of my mind
Something appears then is gone in a flash
A quick smirk, a flutter, a dash.
The walls are thick and hard to climb
...8...9...10...running out of time
A quick look for a familiar landmark
As thoughts sneak about behind me in the dark.
They intertwine like cooked spaghetti
Convoluting like party confetti
A flock of birds with tails of strings
Flying around with broken wings.
I trip and fall and I'm in their nest
When it comes to this game, there's no contest
1..2..3..4...
One more game to even the score.

Balloons

Somewhere in the stratosphere
Lay a collection of forgotten memories.
Afternoons in the park, toes in the sand...
They disappear
One
By
One,
Like balloons floating up to the sky.

A Sonnet in 4/4

The music comes back like an old refrain
A sway of the head, a clap of the hands
Lyrics fall down like droplets of rain
A progression only she understands.
And then, as if she remembered the tune
Her body's alive in perfect tempo
Her voice rings out not a moment too soon
She rises in time with each crescendo.
They say what you know stays with you somehow
Stuck in your head like a favorite song.
Giving you comfort in the here and now
Something familiar to help you along.
Letting the notes simply take her away
The rhythm she lives by every day.

Crumbs

Sometimes I wonder what she's trying to say
As all of her stories change day after day.
Trying to follow the winding trail
Of an ever-growing fisherman's tale.
The recipe is quite unique
For her storytelling technique.
With a little of this and a little of that
New memories form at the drop of a hat.
A beginning from here, an ending from there,
Quite the riddle to crack, if you dare!
Sometimes it returns in a small little burst
Then it all tumbles out in one big outburst.
It's not that she cannot remember,
It's like her thoughts are burning embers -
Struggling to light the flame,
Then just dying out in shame.
Sometimes all you can do is laugh
Hearing her stories being cut in half...
But we all muddle through the best we can
Trying to remember how her story began.
With a helpful nudge, it might come back
Maybe if she just gives her head a smack
She'll rattle something back into place!
Oh, if only that were the case!

Late to the Platform

Each thought is a car moving down a track
Puffing out smoke, not looking back.
Looking for a destination -
A runaway train without a station.
It's like the feeling you have something to say,
Then, just like that, the thought fades away.
The whistle blows with a loud, sharp cough,
And quick as a flash, the train takes off.
A scream in your throat and your hand in the air,
But the train just leaves you standing there.
A little jog to quicken the pace,
But ultimately you're left with soot in the face.

My Mom and Me

There is a monster living inside my head,
Feasting on my fear.
It tap, tap, taps me
Like freezing rain
Just to remind me it's there.
It comes in the quiet hours of the dawn,
Looming in the dark.
Always expected,
Never surprised
When I hear its hateful bark.
It's keen to remind me, when I'm safe and sound,
Of what used to be.
Memories hidden
Away from view
In a glass menagerie.
I try to ignore it when I'm out with friends,
But I feel it pry.
I order a drink
And laugh it off,
But when I'm alone, I cry.
There are times I wish I could just call my mom
When I'm feeling blue,
But I never do
Because I know
That she has a monster, too.
Her monster is strong and smarter than mine,
Feasting on her fear.
And I know it has
A willing host
When another one is near.

(Continued)

It crawls into my brain when it's ravenous
I can hear it chew.
And for every piece
that she loses,
I feel I lose a piece, too.
But we're in this together, my mom and me
Bruised, but carrying on
Stronger together
Fighting the fight
Until our monsters are gone.

What Hurts The Most

The hardest part isn't the forgetting...
It isn't hearing the same story every time
Or even hearing random stories put together.
It isn't the awkward silences or having to explain things
Over and over and over again...
It's having the patience.
It's having the patience to listen to the rants,
Having the emotional strength
To let go.
It's having to try
Over and over and over again...
To remind her of the good.
It's finding the silver lining
With eyes that only see gold.
It's knowing that my mom
Won't know her grandchildren.
And, in time,
Won't know me, either.
It's watching the slow progression,
The loss of hope,
The loss of self,
That hurts the most.

Alternate Reality

In this world, there are no names
There are no rules, there are no games
There's only time, tick, ticking away
Year after year, day after day.
Minutes are hours and days are years
The past is fuel for the Langoliers
Feasting on time as the seconds fly by
They're never fearful, never shy.
The hands of the clock spin freely in time
Never stopping to ring the chime
Never marking the passing day
Just lost in tomorrow and yesterday.

Terminus

There's a place in her brain
Full of lost words
Overpopulated
With forgotten thoughts.
They travel in droves
Packed into subway cars
Bound for
Terminus.
Shoved, shoved, shoved
And sent away
The walls of the cars are scratched
Hopes of freedom.

Stronger Together

We were a full house with no cards to spare
We let all our chips fall down where they may.
But one day The Devil pulled up a chair
And everything changed that warm summer day.
We bet all our money on our best hand:
A pair of hearts and a trio of spades.
But down came the ace, king, queen, jack and ten,
He added our house to his accolades.
But we went all in on the love we had,
We're stronger together when times are tough.
But when we lost again, He took our dad.
With a wink and smirk, He called our bluff.
Again the sly Devil dealt out the cards,
So careful to hide the ace up His sleeve,
Praising His tactic to let down his guard...
His Poker Face poised to have us believe.
But mom was the final heart in our hand,
Backed by three spades and a throwaway card.
For once the game went exactly as planned,
She stood bright and strong as our one safeguard.
The Devil, he gambled on love...and lost.
We're stronger together when times are tough.
With barely a prayer and our fingers crossed,
The battle had ended, we'd had enough.
Mom stood victorious, she'd won the game,
Despite our hand, we found a way to win.
She knows what her family overcame
We're stronger together through thick and thin.

[?]

Inner Conflict

I constantly feel like I'm at war with myself
Two armies bound to collide
On the battleground of my heart.
Shells lie in abundance
Small reminders
Of fiery words said in frustration.
I know this isn't the life she wanted.
Frankly, it's not the life I wanted, either.
How do I overcome the guilt I feel
Planning my own life?
At what point do I stop
Being my mother's mother?
I tiptoe through the sand
Doing my best to avoid land mines.
Walking through the trenches
Battling the ever-changing struggle
Between living for me and living for her.

Big Girl Pants (for my mom)

When I was in grade school, I chopped off my hair
From back length to ear length on a double dog dare
All the boys laughed with mocking chants
And mom said, "Put on your big girl pants!"
When love's first heartbreak left me shattered and torn
Shower-singing "Every Rose Has Its Thorn",
She told me her stories of fleeting romance
And said, "Put on your big girl pants!"
On that hot fall day when I lost my dad
She stood before us, ironclad
Listening to my cries and rants
Saying, "Put on your big girl pants."
When her brain scan came back with a large, dark mass
Spreading and looming like toxic gas
She sat evaluating her new circumstance
And strapped on those big girl pants.
Her courage and bravery are pillars of strength
Keeping us all on the same wavelength
Constantly moving to a changing dance
While flaunting her big girl pants!

Chapter Six: Our Parents

At this point in our life, we often think of our parents. I wonder how they would react to our lifestyle today. Susan and I remember all the sayings our parents had, that we were NEVER going to say. Naturally, we are now quoting them daily.

From my father, William J. McNulty, I truly believe that I carry on his creativity in music and my poetry efforts. Dad loved playing the guitar and singing his songs at family gatherings. He enjoyed the bowling competition. I would like to think he would be proud of my efforts. After a Father's Day visit to St. Michaels, I wrote this verse:

I Can Almost Hear You

I can still hear you sing your song,
We always did our best to sing along.
You wrote the words for the one you love,
Now you look over us from heaven above.
A little country in your voice to hear,
The memories are still near and dear.
From today's dawn to the farthest star,
I still hear the notes from your guitar.
And music now comes from your children's children.
If you were still here, how special it could have been.
And now I have learned some chords to play,
To remember you in my dreams of yesterday.

Mom, Florence Lome McNulty, had this serene presence about her. I try to remember her approach when I am tested beyond what I am comfortable in accepting. Mom had this quiet wisdom about her that said volumes about her. Mom looked for the best in everyone. I wrote a poem for her one Mother's Day and read it to her when we went to visit. Unknown to us at the time, it was the last week of her life. I still remember her tears of appreciation.

This poem was read for Mom at her funeral:

Bittersweet

Today, I think I understand *bittersweet*.
Saying goodbye to Mom is no easy feat.
It's bitter and not something any of us want to do.
I would rather hold your hand while your tea does brew.
But the memories of you will be sweet for all of us to share,
As we all know just how much for your family you did care.
Your soft-spoken words will always be in my ear,
Sharing stories of growing up in the yesteryear.
In the Passover kitchen with your sisters for all to see,
Debating just what was Bubbie's gefilte fish recipe.
The values you gave to each of your children,
Show what will be from what has been.
From your generation to your great grandchildren's generation,
Each new life, in your heart, was a joyful celebration.
Good times and bad times, your children knew you were there.
With a kind word, where to draw the line, or how far to dare.
For almost 92 years, there were words and smiles for the whole family.
Sometimes, no words were needed, just your presence for all to see.
As these words and thoughts now cease,
Our wish for you, Mom, is to rest in peace.

My mother in law, Pearl Solomon Silverman, used to call me her favorite son in law. Of course, I was her only son in law. In the forty plus years I knew her, she often repeated stories and events of decades ago. Susan and I can still retell those tales. Mom set a beautiful table and always served tasty meals. Sunday was for dining out. She set high standards for her family and if you didn't meet them, you heard about it. She was generous to all those within her care. Her love for her children and grandchildren created a special bond.

Jack Silverman was my father in law. Accounting was his trade—both full time and part time on Saturdays. His lesson of doing what you do best, and paying skilled people to handle the tasks they do best still stays with me. Dad had this calm approach to everyday problems and always made problem solving look easy. The only time I ever saw emotion is when we lost our son Stephen. I still remember seeing him cry in our den. In some ways, he was a confidant, especially for the many who came to him seeking advice on taxes and finance issues. There were also bargaining skills I learned from him that still stay with me.

Jack and Pearl

From Palmer Square to Skokie to Winston Towers,
We tell this tale with hearts and flowers.
About Pearl, there is so much that we could say,
And so much more that we can't say on any day.
Her stories of family repeated until we knew them by heart,
And if it was time to entertain, Pearl would always do her part.
Her beautiful grey hair, or was it white?
Pearl & Jack were always quite the sight.
Family dinners were always a wonderful treat,
Tasty and served just right with plenty to eat.
There could be no better father in law than Jack,
When he gave advice it was always right on track.

(Continued)

Sometimes he was the income tax man,
Or there to help with a business plan.
Pearl looking to step out to have a smoke,
Or at the casino with quarters going for broke.
And after dinner with a full tummy,
They always wanted to play gin rummy.
Jack, always there to play games and keep score,
Always with an open mind to listen & explore.
Memories may fade but the lessons taught are still there,
We always think of them, with a smile, love and care.

Available Resources

The amount of information and resources available about dementia or Alzheimer's is seemingly never-ending and always evolving. I wanted to touch on some of the information and encourage you to investigate the wealth of details available online.

If you are a caregiver or if you may become a caregiver, you may want to learn about caregiver support groups. There is a special bond that forms with other caregivers as they are in the same position as you and can easily relate to the issues that you face.

Practical information can be shared to solve problems. You can learn coping skills to handle daily responsibilities. There is someone to talk through challenges and how to manage them. There are resources to discover from other caregivers and how to use them. Often, you can learn solutions that are not in any books.

The Benefits of Exercise

There is much information available showing that exercise offers many benefits as we age.

Regular exercise improves your brain health and keeps your mind working. Self-confidence is improved and you can reduce anxiety and depression. Your memory is improved. Exercise pumps more blood to the brain which improves brain function.

Exercise routines can offer structure for day and improve your ability to handle those activities.

Therapy Dogs

For the 5.3 million that suffer from Alzheimer's disease and the millions more that deal with Dementia, there are trained therapy dogs to assist in their daily activities. They can be constant companions to offer more independence and self-sufficiency. There are fewer mood swings as the dogs can calm bouts of agitation. The dogs relieve depression as the result of loneliness or isolation. The last observation is that a good therapy dog can reignite their interest in the world.

Music Therapy

Many studies show that those suffering from dementia and Alzheimer's benefit from music therapy. It has been shown that those with a musical background have skills that counteract the negative effects of aging such as memory loss and hearing difficulties. Something in music tends to stimulate the brain in patients.

Art Therapy

The benefits of art therapy have shown that this creative process improve one's physical, mental and emotional well-being. This involves the creation of art to increase awareness of self and others. The objective is promote personal development, increase coping skills and enhance cognitive function.

There are art therapists to assist you in this process. Check out what classes are available in your area.

Selecting a Facility

At some point, you may have to pick a facility for a parent or spouse or loved one. How will you proceed? Be aware that there are nursing homes and assisted living facilities that specialize in dementia and Alzheimer's care. If you have long term care insurance, review policy to understand what is covered and amount of reimbursement.

1. Ask others who they would suggest and why. Ask for details or examples of their concerns.
2. Visit the grounds. Are they well maintained? Noise level too much?
3. Visit with the residents. Talk with family members. How does staff interact with patients?
4. What is the resident turnover? What is the staff turnover?
5. Ask about and plan a meal there. Is the food good?
6. Do a safety check. Are there guard rails where needed? How is the staff emergency care?
7. Always inspect what you expect.

What Is the Difference Between Alzheimer's and Typical Age-Related Changes?

Signs of Alzheimer's / dementia	Typical age-related changes
Poor judgment and decision-making	Making a bad decision once in a while
Inability to manage a budget	Missing a monthly payment
Losing track of the date or the season	Forgetting which day it is and remembering it later
Difficulty having a conversation	Sometimes forgetting which word to use
Misplacing things and being unable to retrace steps to find them	Losing things from time to time

What To Do If You Notice These Signs

If you notice any of the warning signs of Alzheimer's in yourself or someone you know, don't ignore them. Schedule an appointment with your doctor.

With early detection, you can:
- Get the maximum benefit from available treatments
- Explore treatments that may provide some relief of symptoms and help you maintain a level of independence longer
- Increase your chances of participating in clinical drug trials that help advance research

Clinical Trials

As information is always changing, please check on line for the latest trial information.

At the end of 2017, there were over 400 clinical trials related to Alzheimer's disease. There are drugs in trials that are showing potential to slow down the progression of Alzheimer's disease. One that has been fast tracked is from AbbVie.

On the web, you can Google "Clinical Trials for Alzheimer's Research" and investigate current progress on drugs that slow down the progression of this disease.

Alzheimer's Association

On the Internet, this resource is located at **https://www.alz.org**.

Here you can locate local chapters, current news, fund raising activities and resources that can benefit you.

Acknowledgements

As with the previous books that we did, I have been blessed with outstanding help.

To my brother, David, for advice and resources.

To my sister, Barbara, for reaching out to market this book.

To Carrie McNulty and Melissa Conner, for their creativity, support and sharing the connection to a parent dealing with this disease.

To Dave Weiner, for editing and shaping this book into a presentable format. Your creative talent is always appreciated.

To Susan: Your input and support always help take my words to the next level. With one look from you, I know that words are worthy of sharing or they need more work.